First Science Experiments

WONDERFUL WEATHER

by Shar Levine and Leslie Johnstone

illustrations by Steve Harpster

Sterling Publishing Co., Inc.
New York

In memory of Gord Fogg, the brother I never had.
I will miss your laughter, friendship, advice and wisdom. —SL

To Shar because I've never dedicated a book to her! —LJ

Edited by Claire Bazinet

Library of Congress Cataloging-in-Publication Data

Levine, Shar, 1953-
  Wonderful weather / Shar Levine & Leslie Johnstone ;
illustrated by
Steve Harpster.
    p. cm. — (First science experiments)
  Includes index.
  ISBN 0-8069-7249-1
  1. Meteorology—Experiments—Juvenile literature. [1.
Weather—Experiments. 2. Experiments.] I. Johnstone, Leslie. II.
Harpster, Steve, ill. III. Title. IV. First science experiments
(Sterling Publishing)
QC863.5 .L49 2003
551.5'078—dc21
                                2002015330

10 9 8 7 6 5 4 3 2 1

Published by Sterling Publishing Company, Inc.
387 Park Avenue South, New York, N.Y. 10016
© 2003 by Shar Levine and Leslie Johnstone
Distributed in Canada by Sterling Publishing
c/o Canadian Manda Group, One Atlantic Avenue, Suite 105
Toronto, Ontario, Canada M6K 3E7
Distributed in Great Britain by Chris Lloyd at Orca Book Services,
Stanley House, Fleets Lane, Poole BH15 3AJ, England.
Distributed in Australia by Capricorn Link (Australia) Pty. Ltd.
P.O. Box 704, Windsor, NSW 2756 Australia

Manufactured in China

Sterling ISBN 0-8069-7247-5

Contents

Note to Parents and Teachers

This book is designed to answer very basic questions young children have about the weather. We can't predict every question but we can get you started satisfying your child's curiosity, and there are loads of free resources available to help.

Studying the weather is one of the easiest and least expensive ways to introduce kids to science. After learning here how to read a thermometer, have your child keep a record of daily temperatures and make up a simple chart of the changes. It's a good way to learn numbers and graphing. Look in a newspaper's weather section to find the place in the world with that day's highest and lowest reported temperatures.

Don't forget to watch how weather affects plants and animals. Weather can be wonderfully entertaining. Each day there's new weather, and new ways of looking at the world around you.

Safety First: These activities are designed to be as safe and as simple as possible. Some adult supervision is suggested with small children, especially when doing experiments in the kitchen, and we've indicated steps that should be only done by an adult. Please read the **Be Safe** checklist given here with your child before starting any of the activities.

Note: Glass breaks, especially in the hands of young children, and thermometers can be very fragile. Avoid those filled with mercury, which is toxic. Look for the less expensive, alcohol-filled kind. The liquid inside is usually dyed red for visibility, while mercury is a metallic-looking silver color.

Be Safe

DO

✔ Before starting, ask an adult if it is okay to do the experiment.

✔ Read through each experiment with an adult first. (It's best if the adult "helps" or stays nearby.)

✔ Have an adult handle anything made of glass or that is sharp. (Thermometers are fragile.)

✔ Keep babies and pets away from experiments and supplies.

✔ Wash your hands after performing all experiments.

✔ Keep your work area clean. Wipe up spills right away.

✔ Tell an adult right away, if you or anyone gets hurt!

DON'T

✔ Don't taste, eat or drink any part of these experiments.

✔ Thermometers are not toys. Do not use a thermometer to take your temperature or the temperature of your friends or pets.

✔ On sunny days, don't go outside without protection, such as a hat and sunscreen.

✔ Never go out during a thunderstorm or dangerous windstorm.

Introduction

It's morning. You wake up and run to the window. Is it snowing or raining? Maybe it's sunny and hot so you can go swimming. Or, brrrr, it's very cold so you need to wear a heavy coat. Whatever's out there, that's weather. Weather happens. But where does weather come from?

Weather is the word we use to describe what's going on in the **atmosphere**, the pocket of air that surrounds our planet. Weather is what it's like now, or will be tomorrow. Look in the newspaper and see if you can find a chart that will tell you what the weather will be over the next 5 days. This is called a **forecast**.

Climate, another weather word, is not the same thing as weather. If you studied the weather over a long period of time for just one place, and recorded for many years what the weather was like each day, you would know the climate for this area.

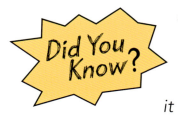

In a desert climate, like the Sahara in North Africa, it hardly ever rains. Animals and plants there have learned to live on very little water. There are no trees or grass for miles and miles, only sand and sky.

The climate is hot in the Amazon rain forest in Brazil, too, but it is wet all year-round. Plants there grow very tall. The plants grow so close together it's hard to take a walk through the forest. Sometimes you can't even see the sky.

Air and Temperature

When you talk about the weather, do you say, "It's cold" or "It's so hot today"? But how hot is it? A thermometer tells us how hot or cold the air is. The temperature goes up or down in steps called degrees (the symbol, °, means degrees).

Many places around the world use a **Celsius** thermometer. On this thermometer, water freezes at 0 degrees and boils at 100 degrees. A very hot day might have a temperature of 40 degrees Celsius, or 40°**C**. If it was -5 degrees Celsius, meaning 5 degrees lower than 0, you might go ice-skating outdoors.

Other places use a **Fahrenheit** scale to measure temperature. On a Fahrenheit thermometer, water boils at 212 degrees and freezes at 32 degrees. A very hot day would measure around 100 degrees Fahrenheit, or 100°**F**, and you could skate outdoors at about 20 degrees. Which scale is used where you live, Celsius or Fahrenheit?

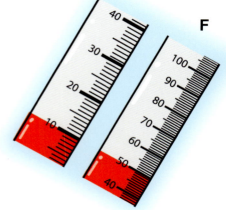

10°C = 50°F

Tip Keep the thermometer away from a hot stove or cold air when you are reading temperatures indoors. When you are reading temperatures outdoors, find some shade. The heat of the sunlight will make the temperature higher than it really is.

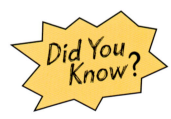

Alcohol is used in thermometers because it doesn't freeze as easily as other liquids. Red coloring makes it easier to see. Some thermometers use a liquid metal called **mercury**. It has a silvery look, but glass thermometers can break....and mercury is poisonous. So always be careful handling thermometers, and only use the kind with a red line in it.

How can I find out what the temperature is ?

Do you remember when you were sick and someone "took your temperature" to see if you had a fever? How do you take the air's temperature? Let's find out.

You need

- indoor/outdoor thermometer (with a red line in it)
- an adult helper
- a watch or clock

Do this

1 Find a thermometer. Be careful. Thermometers are often made of glass and can break. Always ask an adult for help in using one.

2 Hold the thermometer so the **bulb**, the round part, is at the bottom. Do not hold the thermometer by the bulb.

3. Turn the thermometer from side to side, level with your eyes, to find the red line.

4. What number is near the top of the red line? That's the temperature in degrees.

5. Take temperature readings in your room, in the kitchen, even in your bathroom (wait about 5 minutes each time). Have your helper run water from the cold and then hot water taps while you check their temperatures. Go outside and measure the temperature there.

What happened?

The red line may have moved up or down a little when you took the temperature indoors. The warm and cold water made it move more. The temperature outside was probably different from inside your home. If it was winter and cold outside, the line moved down. If it was summer and hot, the line moved up. But what makes a thermometer work?

Liquids **expand**, or take up more room, when they are heated. Very small bits of the liquid, called **molecules**, start to move faster. They need more room so they get farther apart. This pushes the liquid up the thermometer tube, the **stem**. When liquids get colder, they **contract**, or get smaller. The molecules slow down and come closer together. They take up less room, so the liquid slides back down the stem.

Is hot air the same as cold air ?

Liquids expand, or get bigger, when they get hotter. They contract, or get smaller again, as they cool down. Does air do that, too?

You need

- adult helper
- 10-inch (22.5 cm) balloon
- fabric measuring tape
- freezer
- watch or clock
- very warm tap water
- large sink
- baking sheet
- heavy pot

Do this

1. Ask your adult helper to blow up a balloon for you. (Balloons can be hard for kids to blow up. Do not put a balloon in your mouth as you chould choke.) Knot the opening to keep the air inside.

2. Wrap the measuring tape around the middle of the balloon. Write the measurement down.

3 Put the balloon in the freezer for about 5 minutes.

4 Take the balloon out and quickly measure it again. Write the measurement down.

5 Let the balloon warm up, then fill the sink with very warm tap water. Place the balloon in the water.

6 Cover the balloon with the baking sheet. Put the pot on top, to keep the balloon under the water. Wait 5 minutes.

7 Take the balloon out and measure it again.

What happened?

After being in the freezer, the balloon was smaller than when you first measured it. When the balloon was placed in the warm water, it got bigger. The air inside the balloon contracted, or got smaller, when it got colder and expanded, or swelled up, when it got warmer. Like the liquid inside a thermometer, air is made up of tiny particles called molecules. Warm air takes up more space than cool air because the air molecules move farther apart.

Why does my shirt sometimes stick to me on hot days

Have you ever stopped to look at air? "Don't be silly," I hear you say. "Air is invisible. You can't see it." Okay, but let's see if we can find something in the air.

You need
- a mirror with a frame or handle
- refrigerator

Do this

1 Put a mirror into your refrigerator for 10 minutes. Pick up the cold mirror by the frame or handle and bring it up close to your face.

2 Breathe hard onto the mirror.

What happened?

You couldn't see yourself in the mirror because it was fogged up. When you breathed out, **water vapor** moved out of your lungs, too. These molecules of water are so small you can't see them. But when your warm, wet breath hit the cold mirror, the water vapor turned into tiny drops of water. This change from water vapor to the mist on the mirror is called **condensation**.

There's always some water vapor in the air. It's called **humidity**. Sometimes the humidity is high (lots of water) or low (less water). On some hot summer days, the air is really full of water vapor. That's when your shirt feels sticky, and people say, "Whew, it's humid today!" Next time you are outside on a very cold winter day, huff and puff and see if you can "see your breath." That's water vapor!

Water

Water is a big part of weather. It comes down from the sky in the form of rain, snow, hail, or something in between. It's all part of a **water cycle**, a very important part of the world we live in.

Here's how it works. The heat from the sun warms up the Earth and everything on it. When you get out of a pool on a hot day and sit in the sun, the drops of water that cover your body soon disappear. The water has **evaporated**. This means the air has taken the water and turned it into water vapor.

Evaporation is happening all over the world. Water from lakes, oceans, rivers, streams, and even swimming pools is evaporating and moving into the air. The warm wet air moves upward and cools off. That's when clouds form. When there's enough water vapor in the clouds, or when the clouds turn colder, the water turns into drops and falls back to earth in the form of rain or snow. The water fills the lakes, streams, rivers and oceans... and it begins all over again.

Why is the grass wet, when it didn't rain last night ?

If you wake up early on warm summer days, you may find the grass and leaves covered with cold, wet drops of water. It didn't rain, so why are there water drops all over? This water is called **dew**, and it didn't fall from the sky. It's not magic either. It's science!

You need

* a warm day
* tin can with label removed (check for sharp edges)
* water
* crushed ice or ice cubes
* towel

Do this

1 Take the can outside on a warm day. Set it down where it is flat.

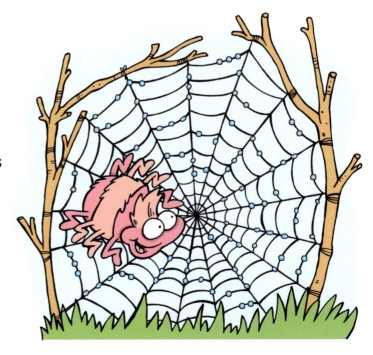

2 Fill the can halfway with water. Dry the outside of the can with a towel.

3 Add ice until the can is filled up. Watch what happens on the outside of the can.

What happened?

Tiny drops of water suddenly appeared. You made dew!

The warm air around the can had water vapor in it. When the air touched the sides of the cold can, it cooled down. This made the water vapor in the cooler air **condense**, turn into liquid, and made dew drops form on the can.

Where do clouds come from?

Look up in the sky. Do you see any clouds? What do they look like? Some clouds are fluffy and white, like cotton balls. Others are dark, almost black, and make you grab an umbrella. At sunrise and sunset, clouds can look red, purple, or yellow—as if they were colored with crayons. But what are clouds anyway?

You can't reach out and touch the clouds, but you can make your own in a bottle.

You need

- an adult helper
- a huge, empty glass jar
- metal strainer
- hot water
- ice cubes

Do this

1 Have your helper fill the jar with hot water, leave it there for two minutes, then pour out most of the water, leaving just an inch or two at the bottom of the jar.

2 It's your turn now. Put the strainer over the mouth of the jar. Fill the strainer with ice cubes. Watch the jar.

What happened?

A cloud formed in the jar! Some of the hot water at the bottom of the jar turned into hot water vapor. The water vapor rose and bumped into the cold air coming off the ice cubes. When the water vapor condensed, it formed a cloud.

Hot air rises and carries with it lots of water vapor. The higher the air rises, the more it cools down. Soon the cold air can't hold all the water vapor so it starts turning into tiny water drops, and becomes a cloud.

Did You Know?

A cloud's color depends on how much water vapor or drops are in it. Some clouds are white because sunlight goes straight through. Black or storm clouds have lots of big water drops in them, so light can't get through. That's why rain clouds sometimes look dark and scary.

Why is the sky blue ?

When you first learned the names of the colors and looked up at the sky, the first question you probably asked was "Why is the sky blue?" What exactly gives the sky its color?

You've made a cloud in a bottle, now here's some blue sky in a glass.

You need

* a helper
* tall, thin glass
* water
* sheet of white paper or cardboard
* flashlight
* whole milk
* tablespoon

Do this

1 Fill a glass with water and place it on a table. Have a helper hold the sheet up behind the glass. (If you don't have a helper, you can prop the sheet up against something.)

2 Turn off all the lights in the room. Shine a flashlight through the water so that the light lands on the white sheet. What do you see there?

3 Add about a tablespoon (15 ml) of milk to the water and shine the light again. What do you see now?

What happened?

The light just went through the plain water onto the sheet. But, when you added milk, the water looked...blue! And the light on the sheet looked pink!

Even though light looks white, it is made up of several different colors. The blue color in light scatters the most, so the light bouncing off the fat molecules in milk looks blue. Red light doesn't scatter as much, so it went through the milk and looked pink, or reddish, on the paper.

The same thing that happened to your water when you added the milk happens to the sky. The light from the sun is scattered by small particles of dust or water vapor in the air, and this makes the sky look blue on a clear, sunny day.

Ice and Snow

Snowflakes are strange things: they are all the same but they are also all different. All snowflakes have six sides, no matter where, no matter when. But, because each snowflake is formed by different conditions, you will never find two that are exactly alike.

Why is that? Water molecules are shaped like triangles. When it's cold enough, and those triangles join together, they form **crystals** with six sides. How a snowflake grows depends on a lot of things: the temperature while it's growing, the amount of water in the air, and how long it takes to make the flake. So each one "grows up" to be just a little bit different.

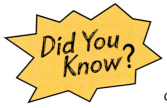

Sleet is not hail; nor is it snow. It's like rain that couldn't decide what it wanted to be. Sleet can happen two ways. Sometimes rain falls through a layer of really cold air, so it freezes a little bit on the way down. Another way you get sleet is when falling snow melts a little on the way down, then re-freezes just before it hits the ground. No matter which way it becomes sleet, it's no fun to be caught outside in a sleet storm.

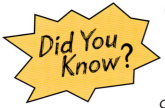

On a clear, cold day, without a cloud in the sky, it can snow! It's called "diamond dust." Tiny ice crystals appear right out of the air. This only happens under very cold temperatures, when it's so cold even the tiniest bit of water vapor in the air condenses and immediately freezes.

Who made those ice pictures on my window ?

It's fun to wake up to ice pictures on your window. But where do they come from? And look, they're *inside* the window!

You find icy **frost** on your windows when it is *very* cold at night and the heat is on inside to keep you warm. But why wait for winter?

You need
- adult helper
- an empty, clean tin can
- crushed ice
- coarse salt (not table salt)
- water
- towel

Do this

1 Fill half the can with crushed ice.

2 Sprinkle a handful of coarse salt on top of the ice.

3 Add enough crushed ice on top of the salt to fill the can.

4 Pour about 1/2 cup (125 ml) of water into the can.

5 Wipe off the outside of the can with the towel, and put the dry can down on a flat surface.

6 Take a big breath of air and puff towards the can.

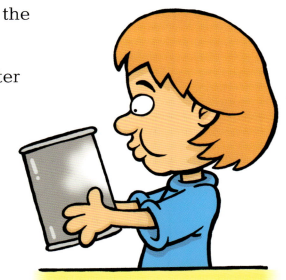

What happened?

You made frost! Your breath made ice patterns on the can.

The ice and salt inside the can made the outside of it *really* cold. The air in the room was warm, and your breath was even warmer. When the room air and your breath hit the can, the water vapor in the air got so cold so fast it turned into frost.

Frost "paints" patterns because snowflakes and frost are a lot alike. The water molecules that touch the icy-cold can are turned into ice crystals. The straight sides of the crystals join together to make patterns—like snowflakes—all over the window.

What is hail ?

Have you ever been caught in a hailstorm? It's like someone in the clouds having a mini-snowball fight with you, but you can't throw back. Where do those hard, little ice-balls come from?

You need

* modeling clay (different colors)
* dental floss or thin wire
* helper

Do this

1 Pull off some modeling clay about the size of a jelly bean. Roll it in your hands until it's round like a small marble.

2 Take a larger piece of another color clay. Flatten it on a table or countertop into a circle. Wrap this clay circle around the clay marble piece so that it covers it completely. You should now have a clay ball the size of a larger marble.

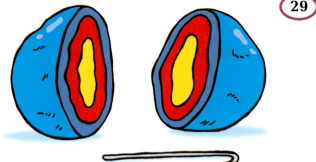

3 If you have other colors of clay, add a few more layers of different colors to the clay ball.

4 Use the piece of dental floss or wire to slice the ball in half. Look at the layers.

What happened?

See the different colored layers inside? Hail is made up of layers, too, but of frozen water. Rising air bounces falling raindrops back up into cold clouds. This turns the raindrops into tiny frozen balls—like that first ball of clay. The frozen balls begin to fall, but they get tossed back up again—like clothes going around in a laundry dryer. Coated with more water, they freeze again and again, until they are so heavy the air can't push them around anymore. That's when they fall to the ground as hard, icy hailstones.

Did You Know?

Hailstorms sometimes damage growing plants. Larger hailstones can weigh over 2 pounds (1 kg)—big enough to break car windshields and hurt people.

Hail is described according to size: from the small pea hail, to golf ball, and grapefruit-size hail.

Why is some snow fluffy and other snow soggy

Rain and snow both fall from the sky, but they are not the same either. Which would you rather shovel?

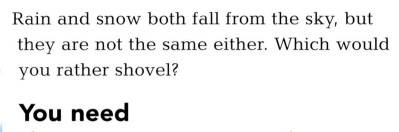

You need

- a straight, clear plastic glass or vase, over 5 inches (12.5 cm) tall
- crushed ice or snow
- measuring cup
- pen or pencil
- paper
- masking tape
- ruler

Do this

1 Stick masking tape up the outside of the glass, from bottom to top.

2 Starting from the bottom of the glass where the water would collect, make a mark every 1 inch (2.5 cm) until you reach the top of the glass. This is a rain gauge. (Put it outside when it rains. Empty it after you measure the amount of rain.)

3 Fill your gauge with 5 inches (12.5 cm) of crushed ice or snow and let it melt. Pour the water into the measuring cup. Write down how much water there is.

4 Now fill the gauge with 5 inches (12.5 cm) of water and pour it into the measuring cup. Write down the amount of water this time.

What happened

From all that snow or ice you only got a little bit of water. That's because water expands when it freezes. And fresh snow, like crushed ice, has a lot of air spaces in it. It takes 5 to 10 times as much snow to make 1 inch (2.5 cm) of rain.

When snow is very cold, it contains less liquid water so the snow is fluffy. It's hard to make snowballs from light fluffy snow. It's the wet water molecules that stick snowballs together. Soggy snow is much wetter. If you use your rain gauge on different kinds of snow, you'll see that soggy snow has much more water than snow that is fine and light. Shoveling really wet snow can make you feel as if you were shoveling rain.

Wind

What is wind? The simple answer is "air on the move." Wind speed is measured in miles or kilometers per hour (mph/kph), the same as speed is measured in cars. But at sea, sailors use the word "knots" (for nautical miles) per hour.

Want to know how fast the wind is blowing? Something called the **Beaufort scale** is used to measure wind. Here is a wind chart to help you tell how fast the wind is blowing.

Easy Wind Chart

1 Do you see smoke? Is it going straight up? Is the flag on a pole not moving at all? There's no wind. **0** mph = zero miles per hour (or **0** kph = zero kilometers per hour).

2 Is smoke drifting a little in one direction? Does it look like maybe the clouds are moving? There's some air movement, maybe **1** to **3** mph (**1** to **5** kph).

3 Can you feel the wind on your face? Can you hear tree leaves rustling? Is the flag moving on the pole? There's a little breeze, probably about **4** to **7** mph (**6** to **11** kph).

4 Now the leaves and small branches are moving more. Small, light flags are waving. Fluffy clouds are moving across the sky. The wind is going maybe **8** to **12** mph (**12** to **19** kph). If you like kites, it's a good time now to run and get it.

5 Dust and papers are blowing around. Smaller tree branches are swaying and flags are flapping in the breeze. The wind is probably about **13** to **18** mph (**20** to **28** kph). Hold onto that kite!

6 Now even small trees are swaying. The wind is moving about **19** to **24** mph (**29** to **38** kph). I hope you have a strong string on your kite.

7 Look! Even bigger tree branches are moving. Things are blowing all around. The wind must be going **25** to **31** mph (**39** to **50** kph)! Kite-flying is too dangerous. It's even hard to stand. We'd better go inside.

Where does wind come from ?

Wind can be wonderful. On hot summer days, a light breeze will cool you down. Wind scatters seeds so that new plants can take root and grow. What makes wind happen?

You need

* adult helper
* paper and pencil
* scissors
* thumbtack
* thread
* clothes hanger
* a heat source

Do this

1 On a piece of paper, have an adult help you draw a spiral shape, then cut it out.

2 Ask your helper to poke a small hole in the center of the spiral with the thumbtack.

3 Push one end of the thread through the hole in the spiral. Tie it. Then attach the other end to a middle of a clothes hanger.

4 Hold or hang the hanger with the spiral several inches above a radiator, a lit table lamp, or even a metal pan heated by the sun. (Don't put the spiral too close to the heat, and take it down when you are finished. Never leave it hanging near heat when you are not there to watch it.)

What happened?

The spiral moved! As the warm air moved upward, it pushed against the underside of the spiral, and made it spin.

It's this upward movement of air that causes winds. As warm air rises, the air pressure under it gets lower and cooler air nearby moves in to take its place. This sideways moving air is wind, and it usually brings a change in the weather.

Which way is the wind blowing?

Sailors need to know wind direction to set their sails to catch the wind and turn their boats safely. Airplane pilots can get an extra "push" flying with the wind. But wind direction helps **meteorologists**, scientists who study the weather, track storms.

You need
* your pointer finger
* glass of water
* a compass

Do this

1 Stick your pointer finger in the water to wet it. Hold your finger up, and blow on your finger. Feel the coolness? Blow again, and look closely at your finger.

2 Now, set your compass down. Turn it so the needle inside is pointing north, toward the letter "N." Stand and face the direction the needle is pointing.

3 Wet your finger again and hold it up so the wind blows on it. When you are ready, read the direction off the compass.

What happened?

The side of the finger you, or the wind, blew on felt cooler. It dried faster, too. When the water started evaporating, turning into water vapor, it used up a lot of heat. The air moved the water vapor away, so more water evaporated. That made it even cooler. By looking at the compass, you could see what direction the wind was coming from.

Did You Know?

Winds are named according to the direction they are coming from. A "north wind" moves from the north towards the south. A wind coming from in-between north and east is called a northeast wind ("nor-easter" for short). Around the world, winds can come from any direction: north, east, south, west; or northeast, northwest, southeast, or southwest.

What makes tornados go around ?

Did you ever flush a toilet just to watch the water go around and down? What has that got to do with tornados? Let's find out.

Note: Do this outside or at least over a sink because it can be messy. If you don't make a watertight seal, you could have a leaky tornado on your hands.

You need

* 2 large plastic pop bottles
* metal washer (to fit pop bottle opening)
* water
* food coloring
* glitter (optional)
* electrical tape

Do this

1 Fill a bottle about 3/4 full of water. Put a drop or two of food coloring in the water. (Add some glitter if you wish.)

2 Put the washer on the opening of the water-filled bottle. Turn the empty bottle upside down on top.

3 Wrap tape around two bottle openings, joining them together. Make sure it is *very* tight!

4 Slide one hand under the water-filled bottle. Put your other hand on the top bottle. Quickly, turn the joined bottles upside down. At the same time, move the joined bottles around in a circle a few times.

What happened?

You made a tornado! A funnel shape called a **vortex** appeared in the top bottle. That's because you moved the bottles in a circle. The vortex let a little bit of air rise up into the top bottle. At the same time, a little bit of water moved down into the bottom bottle...and the air and water kept changing places. The air spinning upward through the water is like the strong winds of a tornado, spinning upward into the sky.

Try the experiment again. Turn the bottles upside down, but this time *don't* move the bottles in a circle. Did you get a tornado?

Thunder and Lightning

Weather can be dangerous. Storms, with their thunder, lightning, strong winds and lots of rain can be scary and cause a lot of damage. When a bad storm is coming, the weather service issues warnings to give people time to get ready (board up windows and go to a safe place). You don't want to be caught outside in dangerous weather.

Did You Know?

*Rain storms called **hurricanes** have strong winds that circle around a low-pressure area. Meteorologists have a hurricane scale. It goes from a low of **1**, with winds from 74 to 95 mph (118 to153 kph), to a high of **5**, with wind speeds greater than 155 mph (250 kph).*

When Storms Come

1 Go inside or find some place to stay during the storm. Getting in a car can protect you from lightning.

2 Don't stand in the open, in a ball field or on a playground. Don't stand under a tree or another tall object. Lightning looks for the tallest thing to hit.

3 Keep away from anything made of metal: like poles, ball field seats, or fences. Lightning is attracted to metal.

4 Stay away from water. Get out of the swimming pool, or off a boat on a lake. It is not safe there. Opening an umbrella can keep off the rain, but it can't protect you from lightning.

5 Don't hold onto metal objects, not even a baseball bat or bike, if a lightning storm is *very* close. How do you know? It's close when the lightning and the thunder happen at *the same time*.

What makes lightning ?

Did you ever think clothes could help you with a science trick? Well, you may be shocked to find lightning there!

You need

* large mirror
* dark room
* nylon stockings, wool sweater, or silk scarf

Do this

1 Find a dark room with a mirror, and leave the light off.

2 Stand in front of the mirror, rub a nylon stocking together. What do you see in the mirror?

3 Do the same thing with a wool sweater or a silk scarf.

What happened?

Tiny sparks flew back and forth around the nylon stocking. It's **static electricity**. The sparks happen when **electrons**, tiny particles too small to see, move through the air. When lots of electrons build up in one place or on one thing, some will jump...and give off a static charge. This can happen when you take laundry out of the drier, or try to separate your socks.

On hot and humid days, lots of warm wet air sometimes moves upward very quickly. It forms clouds, and the temperature inside gets very cold. The very fast-moving air causes an electric **charge** to build up. The electricity builds up until the cloud can't hold it anymore. So it **discharges**, or moves out suddenly. That's when you get the bright "flash" of lightning and the "boom" that is thunder. Lightning is just one really big electrical discharge.

Did You Know?

The NASA website and some weather channels show lightning strikes around the world. It's hard to believe but, just while you were reading these few words, there were probably over 100 lightning flashes taking place somewhere on Earth!

What makes thunder ?

Thunderstorms can shake your house and make your dog run and hide. But what causes that loud "boom"? How about making your own thunder? It's not as loud, but you won't have to go out in a storm.

You need

⭐ a small paper bag   ⭐ a hard surface

Do this

1 Gather the opening of the paper bag together, like a little sack. Blow into the bag, then close the opening tightly to keep the air inside.

2 Smash the bottom of the bag against a table. Don't let go of the bag while you do this! Keep the air trapped inside. What did you hear? Was that thunder?

What happened?

When the bag "popped" open there was a loud noise. While this noise didn't rattle your windows, you did make mini-thunder. It happened because the air inside rushed out when the bag broke open.

In the clouds, the "boom" is caused by the sudden rush of air outward too, after being heated by the lightning flash. When a lightning storm is very near, sometimes you can hear a crackling sound—almost like the "tearing" sound of the paper bag—just before the loud boom or crash.

Lightning and thunder are a team. The bigger the lightning flash, the louder and longer the sound of thunder. They happen at the same time, but you always see the lightning before you hear the thunder. Why? Because light (the lightning) travels faster than sound (the thunder). They *seem* to happen at different times, but it's just that the light reaches your eyes before the sound reaches your ears.

where do rainbows come from ?

If the sun shines right after a rain, look and you may be lucky enough to see a rainbow. But you don't need to wait for rain to see a rainbow. You can make your own.

You need

- a sunny day
- shallow glass baking dish
- a mirror
- water
- adult helper
- white paper or cardboard

Do this

1 Put the glass baking dish flat on the ground or a table.

2 Place the mirror in the dish. Lean it up against one side.

3 Turn the dish so the mirror faces the sun.

4 Add water until the dish is about half full.

5 Ask your helper to hold up the paper at the end of the dish away from the mirror and move it around slowly. Watch for the sunlight bouncing off the mirror.

What happened?

A rainbow appeared! The water in the dish bent the sunlight. Even though sunlight looks white, it has colors in it. And when the light is bent, it breaks up into red, orange, yellow, green, blue, indigo (a purplish color) and violet. This is called **refraction**. It's how white sunlight puts a rainbow on the paper.

After a rain, lots of small drops are still in the air. When sunlight hits the drops, the light bends to make a rainbow, just like the rainbow you made.

Did You Know?

Some people say there is a pot of gold at the end of a rainbow. Don't start off to find it, because you never will. Every time you move, your rainbow moves, too. The light that makes up the rainbow you see will shine through different water drops. That's why no two people can see the exact same rainbow; only their own personal one.

Index